BOOK ANALYSIS

Written by Daphné Troniseck
Translated by Emma Lunt

Q & A

BY VIKAS SWARUP

Bright
≡**Summaries**.com

VIKAS SWARUP   1

Indian writer and diplomat

Q & A   2

A dark yet colourful depiction of modern India

SUMMARY   3

An uneducated waiter becomes a billionaire
Bad luck in Mumbai
Fleeing to Agra
Who Wants to Be a Millionaire?

CHARACTER STUDY   8

Ram Mohammad Thomas
Nita
Gudiya Shantaram/Smita Shah
Salim Ilyasi
Prem Kumar
Shankar

ANALYSIS   14

India, a different country
The world of Bollywood
Slumdog Millionaire: from book to film

FURTHER REFLECTION   20

Some questions to think about...

FURTHER READING   22

VIKAS SWARUP

INDIAN WRITER AND DIPLOMAT

- **Born in Allahabad (India) in 1961 or 1963**
- **Notable works:**
  - *Q & A* (2005), novel
  - *Six Suspects* (2008), novel
  - *The Accidental Apprentice* (2014), novel

Vikas Swarup was born in the early 1960s and grew up in a family of lawyers before embarking on a career in diplomacy. Within this field, he deals particularly with Turkey, the United States, Great Britain and South Africa. Since 2013, he has been working at the Ministry of External Affairs in New Delhi, where he lives with his wife, an artist, and their two sons.

Swarup used his imagination and creativity to write his three novels. His books are all bestsellers that have been awarded numerous prizes, translated into dozens of languages and adapted for cinema. This sizeable success can be explained in particular by the fascination that Indian culture holds over the rest of the world.

Q & A

A DARK YET COLOURFUL DEPICTION OF MODERN INDIA

- **Genre:** novel
- **Reference edition:** Swarup, V. (2005) *Q & A*. New York: Simon & Schuster.
- **First edition:** 2005
- **Themes:** modern India, love, quiz show, luck

Q & A, which was published in 2005, is Vikas Swarup's debut novel. It tells the story of Ram Mohammad Thomas, a young, uneducated 18-year-old waiter, who wins a general knowledge quiz show and pockets the astronomical sum of one billion rupees. Accused of cheating, he is ordered to explain himself in order to prove his innocence.

The novel, which has been translated into 43 languages, quickly became a bestseller and received many literary awards, including South Africa's Exclusive Books Boeke Prize in 2006 and the *Prix Grand Public* at the Paris Book Fair in 2007. The following year, Swarup's story was brought to the big screen by the British director Danny Boyle, under the title *Slumdog Millionaire*. The film received many awards, including eight Oscars, two of which were for Best Film and Best Director.

SUMMARY

AN UNEDUCATED WAITER BECOMES A BILLIONAIRE

In the Indian version of *Who Wants to Be a Millionaire*, a new programme appears promising to give one billion rupees to anybody who can correctly answer the questions they are asked. The first contestant, Ram Mohammad Thomas, is a humble 18-year-old waiter who is struggling to survive in a socially divided modern India that is marked by violence. He does not have the ideal profile to win the game; nonetheless, his performance is flawless and he wins the jackpot.

But the game show producers did not expect somebody to win the money so quickly; they still need eight months to clear the debt of producing the programme. Furthermore, they are convinced that Ram cheated. Their suspicions lead the young man to be secretly tortured by the police to force him to confess and to sign a declaration renouncing his win. A lawyer, Smita Shah, then shows up and, although Ram does not know her, she offers to defend him and takes him out of this forceful interrogation. When she asks him how he managed to win, he replies "Well, wasn't I lucky that they asked only those questions to which I knew the answers?" (p. 17). A long confession then begins, which dives into Ram's past and explains why he knew the answers to the questions that he had been asked. Each question, based on general knowledge relating to India (its history, norms, culture, etc.), refers to a chapter of his life.

BAD LUCK IN MUMBAI

After being abandoned when he was just a baby, Ram lived with a priest. When Ram was eight, the priest died, and the young boy was sent to a reform school rather than being placed in an adoption centre, because he was already too old to be adopted. Situated in Delhi, it is "a crumbling house where you are forced to live in a crowded dormitory with dozens of other kids" (p. 73). The children there do not have enough food, as the cook resells the meat that is meant for them to restaurants. After contracting jaundice, Ram is quarantined alone in a bedroom. A new patient soon joins him. It is Salim, a young Muslim boy who ended up at the institution after seeing his family burned alive by Hindus. The two boys become best friends.

One day, Babu Pillai, a notorious crook, invites Ram and Salim to his school in Mumbai, allowing them to leave the reform school. They are isolated so that they can be trained in sacred Hindu songs, and barely see the other children, who are all ill. But Ram realises that the schoolchildren must beg and that they have been mutilated to inspire pity from passers-by. He then overhears a conversation about the two of them: "Send them out on the trains from next week. We will do them tonight. After dinner." (p. 97). Realising that their time has come to be mutilated, Ram and Salim manage to escape in the nick of time.

The two boys have to work and conveniently remember that one of Babu Pillai's young patients often goes to the house of Neelima Kumari, a retired 'Tragedy Queen' who had taken pity on him and who was looking for a servant. Ram applies and is given the position. He can then move into a *chawl* with Salim, a "bundle of one-room tenements occupied by the lower middle classes" (p. 56). But, after the actress commits suicide, probably due to her difficulties with a violent lover who beat her, Ram is forced to work at a foundry.

One day, Salim and Ram see their new neighbours arrive. Mr Shantaram is a renowned scientist who studies stars and who has been an alcoholic since one of his astronomy colleagues stole his discovery. He is incapable of holding down a long-term job due to his alcoholism and so, having spent all his savings, he is forced to move into the *chawl* with his family. Mr Shantaram is a violent man who beats his wife and his daughter Gudiya. Ram supports the girl by holding her hand through a hole between their two homes. The walls are not very thick and, one day, Ram hears Mr Shantaram trying to rape his daughter. When he sees him stumbling back home the following day, Ram jumps at him and the wobbly guardrail breaks under his weight, causing Mr Shantaram to fall down several storeys. Convinced that he has killed the man, Ram flees.

FLEEING TO AGRA

When he arrives in Agra, Ram becomes a tour guide at the Taj Mahal. After one of his visits, some very rich Indian students bring him to the red-light district where he meets Nita, a prostitute with whom he falls madly in love. Nita feels the same but her pimp, who is also her brother, demands a fortune from Ram to buy her freedom.

After the death of his friend Shankar, a young man whom he met in Agra and who was killed by a rabid dog, Ram learns that Nita has been hospitalised. A man mutilated, beat and burned her with a cigarette. He immediately recognises – as much physically as by the way he acts – the man who emotionally destroyed Neelima Kumari by inflicting the same abuse: it is the television presenter Prem Kumar. Wanting to save Nita at any cost, Ram steals the money necessary to buy her freedom from Shankar's mother, a rich princess. When he arrives at the hospital, he drops the money on the ground, and a man who is present at the scene calls out to him: his son has rabies and is on the brink of death. He asks Ram to give him the money so that he can buy the vaccine to save his life. Ram does not listen and goes to Nita's bedroom.

But her brother asks him for more money than expected, stating that it is because of him that Nita is in this state and that he must also pay her hospital fees. Aggrieved, Ram gives the money to the father of the dying boy, who reminds him of Shankar. It is then that he notices an advertisement in a magazine asking people to sign up for the quiz show *Who Wants to Be a Millionaire?*, with a photograph of its famous host, Prem Kumar. His decision is made. He is going to return to Mumbai.

WHO WANTS TO BE A MILLIONAIRE?

During the advert break before the final question of the quiz, Ram goes to the toilet with the presenter, Prem Kumar. Indeed, he has recognised him: he is the man who attacked

Neelima Kumari and Nita. Ram threatens him with a gun, but he is not a killer and does not manage to pull the trigger, realising that he cannot kill somebody in cold blood, even scum like Prem Kumar.

In exchange for his mercy, Prem Kumar gives him a clue about the answer to the final question. When he returns to the stage, Ram plays the game by firstly using his final life-line (Phone-a-Friend), then tosses his lucky coin to decide the answer to the question, which turns out to be correct.

At the end of his confession, the lawyer Smita reveals her true identity to Ram: she is none other than Gudiya, Mr Shantaram's daughter, whom he thought he had killed. He actually only broke his leg and never touched his daughter again after that episode. Gudiya has done everything to find Ram and to thank him. She saves him as he saved her years before.

CHARACTER STUDY

RAM MOHAMMAD THOMAS

Ram, the youngest and only winner of the new quiz show *Who Wants to Be a Millionaire?*, is an uneducated 18-year-old waiter. This orphan was abandoned in the evening of Christmas Day outside the Church of St Mary in Delhi. Taken in by Father Timothy after being abandoned for a second time by a couple who had adopted him, he has a happy childhood until the priest's death.

Men from the interfaith committee come to ensure that Father Timothy has really adopted the young orphan. In order to avoid a riot or the vandalism of his church (relations between different religious communities are tense), these representatives suggest renaming the child, whom Father Timothy had baptised Joseph Mickael Thomas. They consider this name to be too Christian and not reflective of the diversity of India. In order to avoid angering any religious community, Father Thomas gives him the new name of Ram (a Hindu name) Mohammad (a Muslim name) Thomas (a Christian name which he keeps from the first couple who adopted him). Luckily the Sikh representative was absent that day...

Despite the numerous challenges he faces, Ram always proves to be very generous towards the weak. When he earns a decent living in Agra by giving tours of the Taj Mahal, he constantly lends money to his friends, even though he knows full well that he will never get it back. Furthermore, when he earns 50 000 rupees after working for a rich family in Delhi, his first thought is to go back to Mumbai and share it Salim. One last example: after stealing money to buy back Nita's freedom and facing her brother's refusal, Ram offers the money to a man whose son will die of rabies if he does not get the life-saving vaccine.

Ram is also a very, perhaps even overly, curious man. But this character flaw enables him to save Salim from the clutches of Gupta, the assistant director of the reform school who was preparing to sexually abuse him. It is also his curiosity that drives him to listen through the wall that separates the bedrooms at the *chawl* and enables him to learn that Mr Shantaram is assaulting his wife and his daughter Gudiya. Ram thus offers brotherly support to the young girl.

Ram has never been attracted by money. He is aware that being rich is far from being happy. His only wish is to be able to eat and pay for housing. What else could he, a stupid orphan, hope for? When he signs up for *Who Wants to Be a Millionaire?*, he is not looking for money but revenge. He recognises Prem Kumar, the programme's presenter, as the man who attacked both Nita and Neelima Kumari. He decides to participate in order to kill the man, while luck enables him to answer all the quiz questions correctly.

In the epilogue, we discover that generosity still guides his actions: he frees the beggar children that are oppressed by Babu Pillai's associates, passes himself off as a producer by financing the film in which Salim takes the lead role, so that he can realise his dream of becoming an actor, and buys the freedom of Nita, whom he marries.

In the end, all the challenges that the young hero faces are not in vain: they enable him to find love, keep his friends and win enough money to do good for those around him. As a prize for his kindness, all the elements come together so that he finally has a happy existence. "Luck comes from within" (p. 318): these are Ram's final words which conclude the story in which the good and the bad that every individual does has an impact on their entire life.

NITA

Nita is a prostitute who lives in Agra. Ram meets her when he is working as a tourist guide at the Taj Mahal and a group of students invite him to the red-light district. Initially considering him to be one client among others, Nita does not allow him to get close but, little by little, their relationship intensifies and they fall madly in love with one another.

But Nita is not free; she belongs to her pimp, who is none other than her brother. She did not choose her job as a prostitute herself, but was forced into it by her family: in certain Indian religions, young women within a family are raised with this goal. Indeed, this is why she does not like being told she is pretty. Her family chose her to be a prostitute over her sister because of her beauty. The cost of her freedom is 400 000 rupees, a sum that Ram can only pay after winning the quiz show.

GUDIYA SHANTARAM/SMITA SHAH

Smita is a lawyer who gets Ram out of a violent interrogation after his victory on the quiz show. If he wants her to help him, he must first tell her his story.

At the end of the story, Smita reveals her true identity. Her name is Gudiya, and she is the young girl that Ram supported when her drunk father was abusing her. She tells him that he did not kill her father by causing him to fall down the stairwell and that he escaped with only a broken leg. Since then, he has never beaten her again.

Gudiya set her mind on finding Ram to return the favour. She worked hard at school and became a lawyer, while trying to track down Ram. One day, she happened to fall upon his file and rushed to help him. Thanks to her, Ram receives the billion rupees and lives comfortably for the rest of his life. They are connected by a strong friendship, which began in childhood.

SALIM ILYASI

Salim, a candid and very naïve young man, is Ram's best friend. Orphaned at the age of 7, he watched his family die, burned alive by Hindus due to their Muslim beliefs. He meets Ram at the reform school which he is sent to after this tragedy. They are connected by a strong friendship: together, they escaped from Babu Pillai, just before being subjected to the mutilation that would have condemned them to begging.

Salim is a lively and intelligent child. He sings well and learns the sacred songs quickly during their training at Babu Pillai's home. He becomes a resourceful young man, seizing every opportunity that could lead to his dream of becoming an actor. Indeed, he is fanatical about Bollywood cinema. He and Ram hop from one obscure screen to another to watch films from this genre.

Once a billionaire, Ram makes his best friend's dream come true by offering him the lead role in a film that he is financing, without revealing that this opportunity has come from him.

PREM KUMAR

Prem Kumar is the presenter of *Who Wants to Be a Millionaire?*. He is a violent man who enjoys harming women and is involved in rather sleazy matters. It is due to the fact that he presents the quiz show that Ram decides to sign up with the aim of killing him. He has in fact recognised him as the attacker of Neelima Kumari and his beloved Nita.

Prem Kumar is an unbearable character. He tries multiple times to trip Ram up or simply changes the question during the quiz to try to cause him to lose the money he has already won. Before the end of the quiz, Ram follows him to the toilet, threatens him with a gun and confesses that he knows about his wrongdoings. In order to be spared, he gives Ram a clue that enables him to correctly answer the last question. He is found dead two months later, probably having been assassinated by the crooks who produced the programme.

SHANKAR

Shankar is the first person that Ram meets in Agra. He is the one that brings Ram to Princess Swapna Devi's palace where Ram, like Shankar, rents a bedroom in the attic. Shankar is in fact the princess's illegitimate son, whom she refuses to recognise. He does not have to work for her, but is just about tolerated and has to take care of himself to survive. Shankar is a young man with a talent for drawing and he is very kind. When he arrives in Agra, Ram does not have a penny to his name and cannot find anywhere to live. It is Shankar who houses him in his bedroom until he finds a job.

He speaks in code which means that nobody can understand what he is saying. During his childhood, he suffered a trauma when he learnt who his mother was. At night, he calls out to her in his dreams and it is only during these moments that he expresses himself normally. His subconscious probably blocks rational language as a reaction to his mother's rejection.

Shankar is killed by a rabid dog and Ram, having discovered his secret in the drawings that he took great care of, asks his mother to give him money to buy the vaccine that could save his life. But she refuses, and Ram looks after Shankar, who dies in terrible pain, until the very end. Outraged by the princess's indifference, Ram breaks into her palace during a dinner and leaves Shankar's dead body on the table among the guests.

ANALYSIS

INDIA, A DIFFERENT COUNTRY

India was under colonial British domination from the mid-18th century and, since acquiring its independence in 1947, it has not stopped fighting to conserve its culture and traditions. According to statistics, the country is self-sufficient, meaning that it can produce everything it needs and does not need to import any goods whatsoever, including food. Being the second most populous country in the world (with 1.2 billion inhabitants) after China, India takes steps to avoid the saturation of its land: a policy that limits births has been implemented and contraception by sterilisation is encouraged.

India was the first South Asian country to open its elections to universal suffrage in 1952, which is why it is considered the 'largest democracy in the world', despite the rather high level of illiteracy within the population. While India is also presented as the non-violent country, its torchbearer, Mahatma Gandhi (political leader and spiritual guide, 1869-1948) was assassinated by Hindus who found him too tolerant of Muslims. Violence between the different religions that must live together has always existed, but social violence and corruption are also rife and corrupt the country even more, as does the exploitation of lower castes (or the 'outcastes') by higher castes. Moreover, nationalism among Hindus and Muslims alike is intensifying, creating many conflicts between these communities in a country that is practically the size of a continent and that comprises almost as many cultures as the whole of Europe.

Despite everything, this cultural diversity represents great wealth for the country. A clearer distinction can be established between the population in the north, who have been influenced by the West, and those in the south, known as Dravidians, who form a separate linguistic family. These categories are not set in stone and still contain many different religions (Hinduism, Buddhism, Islam, Jainism, Catholicism, Sikhism, etc.) which have also enabled the development of many philosophies. As well as this ethnic and religious diversity, India must come to terms with a rather rigid caste system, despite its legal abolition by the Constitution in 1950, which proclaimed India as a secular republic where all inhabitants should be equal.

CASTES

Castes are based on the principle a hierarchy inherited from the ancient societies of the Indian subcontinent. Their roots lie in Hinduism, but they affect the entire Indian population, regardless of their religious beliefs. Although the Constitution banned it, this system remains deeply rooted in contemporary society and gives rise to many injustices. There are four main hierarchised castes: the Brahmins, comprising priests and teachers; the Kshatriyas, who are warriors; the Vashiyas, composed of traders; and the Shudras, which refers to servants. There is also a fifth caste, the Dalits, formerly known as 'untouchables', which encompasses all people who do the most unclean jobs (such as butchers) and who are therefore 'impure'. They are considered 'outcastes' in India and cannot aim for anything.

Endogamy is a fundamental principal of this system, and involves members of a caste belonging to this caste for their entire life and marrying among themselves, limiting interactions with other social classes as much as possible. Castes are associated with a career, although this match is not absolute due to the appearance of many new jobs.

This social diversity and the rigidity of the caste system are particularly exploited in the novel, particularly in the description of Mumbai, which was previously called Bombay. It is the most populous Indian city and one of the most saturated cities on earth. Here we find all social classes: the rich own the buildings, a symbol of the city's economic success, while the majority of the poorest families live in slums where they are piled into tiny, unsanitary housing.

THE WORLD OF BOLLYWOOD

Bollywood (which comes from 'Bombay' and 'Hollywood') is the name given to the successful industry of Indian cinema produced in Mumbai and performed in Hindi (which is the most spoken language in India). This popular film genre makes the country to the top consumer and producer of films in the world, with 15 million viewers per day and 1 200 films produced per year, of all genres. However, the term 'Bollywood' has a bad reputation in India because it is too similar to Hollywood, from which India wishes to detach itself by producing films that do not follow the same style as American blockbusters. Nonetheless, the genre has largely drawn on Hollywood films, while preserving its own norms and its particular identity. It is characterised by its style which is close to a musical, with many scenes being sung and/or danced.

Bollywood cinema is now exported to almost every country in the world, by emphasising its rather exotic style which holds a certain fascination over Western audiences. It is the image of a changing India, with one side anchored in secular values and cultural traditions and the other accelerating towards modernisation at dizzying speed. Cinema has found a certain balance between the two by presenting what Indians expect from the modern world while suppressing the frustrations they are struggling with. Cinema therefore takes on an important social role, which explains its immense success in the country.

The main themes that are dealt with are the weight of conventions and impossible love between different castes. The kitsch and colourful décor, wild dances, lively music and exaggerated characters are made to maintain the illusion and to anchor the story in unreality. In most films, characters are freed of social pressure and overcome the idea of caste, which is allowed because it is fictional.

Swarup's novel refers to this universe particularly through the dream that drives Salim to become a Bollywood cinema star, but also through similar themes that he depicts.

SLUMDOG MILLIONAIRE: FROM BOOK TO FILM

When Tessa Ross, the director of the film and telefilm department at the British television channel Channel 4, read the draft of Vikas Swarup's novel before it had even been edited, she requested the rights to adapt it for cinema. Indeed, she immediately sensed the interest of this novel which emphasises a little-known reality in Western society: the increasingly clear disparities in India between the poor who live in slums and an emerging crowd of 'nouveau riches'.

But adapting a book to make a film version is not an easy task, especially as the novel does not follow its hero's life in a linear way. In fact, it is made up of 12 chapters which each deal with a particular episode in Ram's life and are constructed in a disjointed fashion. Some of them can be compared to short stories which have no connection with the main characters. At the end of each chapter, we return to the quiz show where the episode of Ram's life that he has just described enables him to answer a question.

It was the British director Danny Boyle (born 1956) who made the film, and he made it into a comedy which borders on a fairy tale, in which we go from laughing to crying. Returning to the quiz show at the end of each episode of Ram's life allows for a blend of genres and gives the film a certain rhythm. Furthermore, unlike an Indian filmmaker who would perhaps have not granted attention to certain details, the English director, who was a stranger to Indian culture, was able to bring a new and external view and a completely different energy to the film.

The screenplay takes certain liberties regarding the original text, particularly when it comes to the protagonists. Ram and Salim are no longer friends, but brothers, and Salim is a negative character who brings Ram down. The character of Nita, Ram's fiancée, appears much sooner in the film, and the character of Gudiya/Smita has simply been removed. While in Swarup's story, Ram plays the quiz show with the intention of avenging Nita and doing good for those around him, it is the lure of money that attracts the young man in the film version. The area where the two medias meet is on the message transmitted: to get to know India in the slums and its contrasts.

After being released in cinemas in October 2008, *Slumdog Millionaire* was met with resounding success around the world. It won many awards, including seven BAFTAs (British Academy of Film and Television Arts), four Golden Globes and no less than eight Oscars in 2009. Proof, if you need it, of the fascination India holds over the rest of the world.

FURTHER REFLECTION

SOME QUESTIONS TO THINK ABOUT...

- Vikas Swarup opts for a non-chronological chain of events in his novel. What effect does this choice have?
- Why does Ram receive names from different religions?
- Ram gets rid of his lucky coin at the end of the novel. What do you think this gesture means?
- Why does Prem Kumar try to mislead Ram during the quiz show?
- When Ram is pointing his gun at Prem Kumar, what stops him for pulling the trigger?
- Do you think that Ram deserved to win the billion rupees, considering Prem Kumar gave him a clue about the last question? Justify your answer.
- What message is Vikas Swarup looking for share by telling the story of this young man who suffers a series of misfortunes and sees his life turned upside down overnight?
- Why is modern India struggling to abolish castes? Develop your answer.
- If Ram belonged to a caste, which do you think it would be? Develop your answer.
- Popular Bollywood cinema holds a certain fascination as much over Indian audiences as Western audiences. What are the reasons for its success? Are they the same for Indians and Westerners? Develop your answer.
- Why was the film adaptation of this novel so popular? Develop your answer.

We want to hear from you!
Leave a comment on your online library
and share your favourite books on social media!

FURTHER READING

REFERENCE EDITION

- Swarup, V. (2005) *Q & A*. New York: Simon & Schuster.

ADAPTATIONS

- *Slumdog Millionaire*. (2008) [Film]. Danny Boyle. Dir. UK/ USA: Warner Bros.

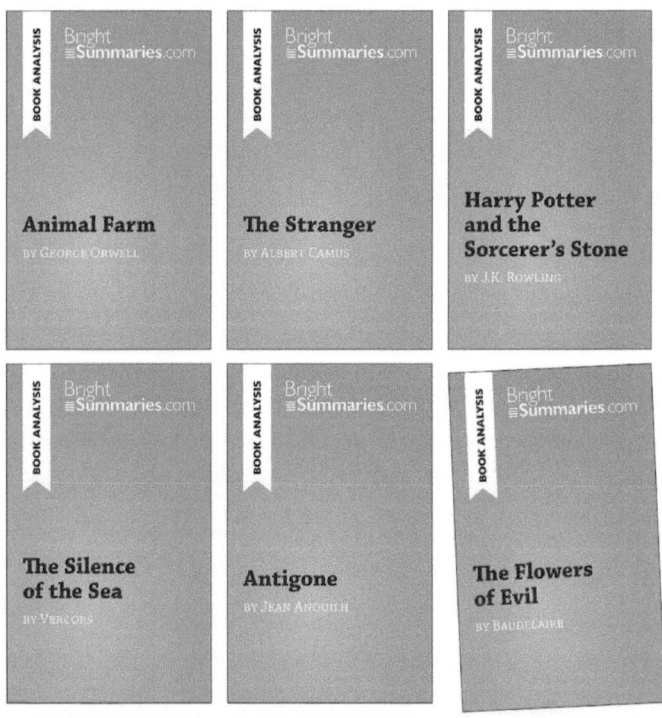

Ebook EAN: 9782806294104

Paperback EAN: 9782806294128

Legal Deposit: D/2017/12603/89

Cover: © Primento

Digital conception by Primento, the digital partner of publishers.